W9-BRM-059

Count Your Way through Korea

by Jim Haskins

illustrations by Dennis Hockerman

Carolrhoda Books, Inc./Minneapolis

To Michael and Marcus

LIBRARY OF CONGRESS CATALOGING-IN-PUBLICATION DATA

Haskins, James, 1941-
Count your way through Korea / by Jim Haskins ; illustrations by Dennis Hockerman.
p. cm.
Summary: Presents the numbers one to ten in Korean, using each number to introduce concepts about Korea and its culture.
ISBN 0-87614-348-6
1. Korea—Civilization—Juvenile literature. 2. Counting—Juvenile literature. 3. Korean language—Numerals—Juvenile literature. [1. Korea. 2. Counting.] I. Hockerman, Dennis, ill. II. Title.
DS904.H29 1989
951.9—dc19 88-25897
CIP
AC

Manufactured in the United States of America

1 2 3 4 5 6 7 8 9 10 99 98 97 96 95 94 93 92 91 90 89

Introductory Note

The Korean language is part of a family of languages called Altaic, which also includes Turkish and Mongolian. It is not related to Chinese. But centuries of close contact between Korea and China have added many Chinese words to the Korean language.

Koreans use two different kinds of numbering systems. One is called Sino-Korean, which means it is influenced by Chinese. The other is Korean. Sino-Korean numbers are used to count minutes and money. Korean numbers are used to count persons and things. The Korean numbers are used in this book, because in this book we count persons and things.

The Korean language contains some vowels that are pronounced differently than in English. The sound ŏ is often pronounced like the *u* in the English word *but*.

1 하나

(hah-NAH)

The **one** building that is most symbolic of Korea is Ch'omsŏngdae (chom-sung-DEH). It is a stone astronomical observatory, or building where people study the stars and planets in the sky. It is thought to be the oldest existing observatory in the world. It is often pictured on travel posters, in guidebooks, and on postage stamps.

Ch'omsŏngdae stands 29 feet tall and is shaped like the top part of a glass bottle. It is made up of 365 stones, one stone for each day in a year. The observatory was built in the seventh century during the reign of Queen Sondok. Heavenly signs and what people say they mean are still very important in Korean culture.

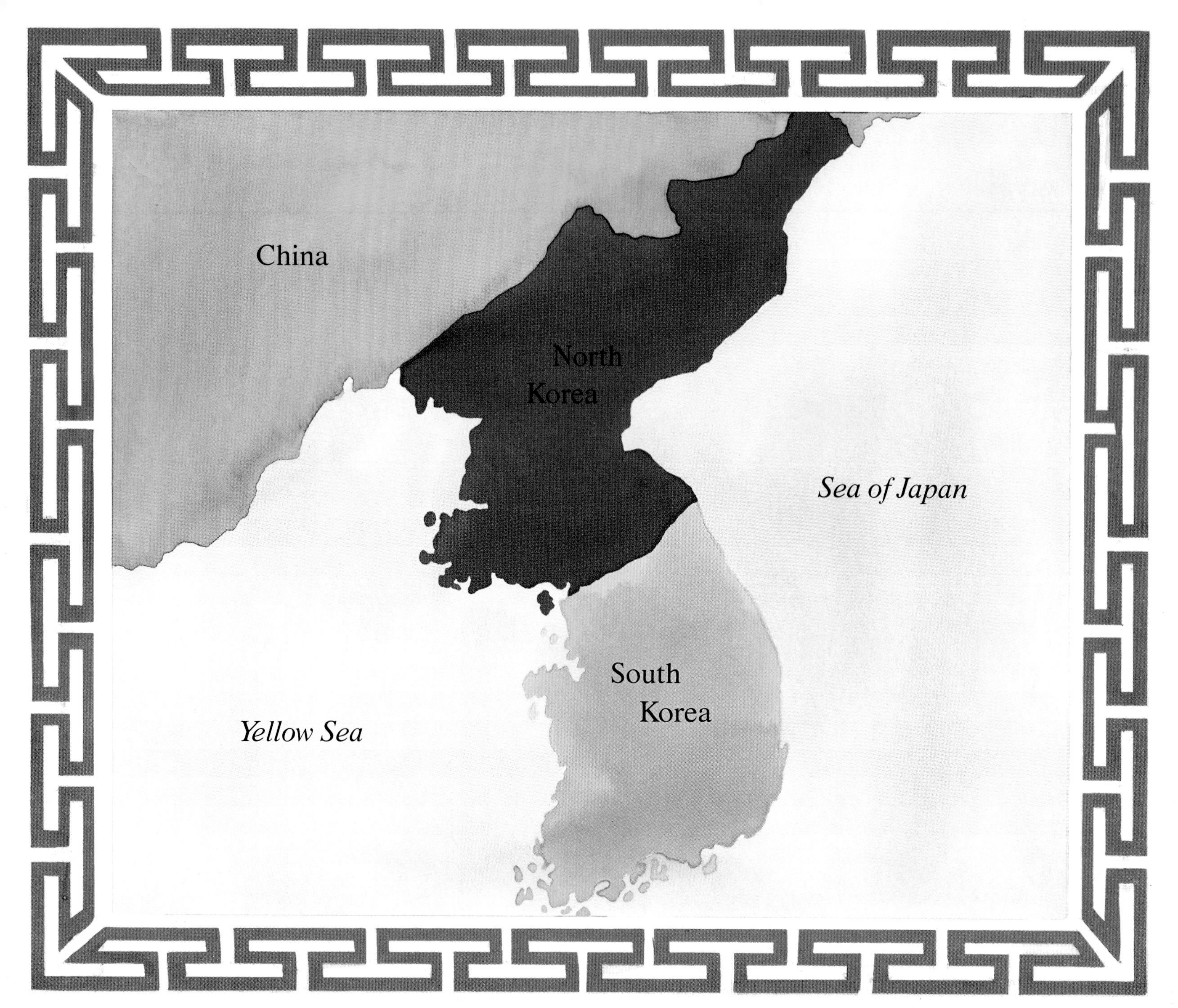
China
North
Korea
Sea of Japan
South
Korea
Yellow Sea

2 둘 (tool)

There are **two** Koreas, North and South. North Korea is called the Democratic People's Republic of Korea. South Korea is called the Republic of Korea. The country was divided in 1948, after World War II. The two regions could not agree about how Korea should be governed.

All attempts to reunite the country, both by force and by treaty, have failed. Both Koreas are now independent nations. Most of the information in this book is about South Korea.

3 셋 (set)

Three people are required for Korean seesaw, which is a game usually played by girls. They traditionally play seesaw to celebrate the Korean New Year's Day.

Playing the Korean version of seesaw requires good balance. The players at either end of the long plank stand, rather than sit, and one is thrown up into the air as the other goes down on the opposite end. The third player, who sits in the middle, keeps the plank in place.

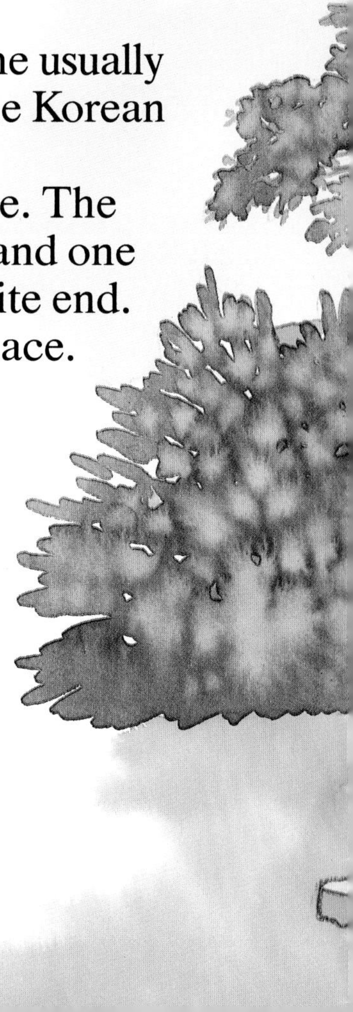

4 넷
(net)

There are **four** parts to the traditional costume for men in Korea: a short, loose-fitting shirt with long sleeves, called a *chŏgori* (cho-GO-ree); a vest worn over the shirt; baggy pants, called *paji* (BAH-jee), that are tied at the ankles; and a hat. The most traditional hat is made of stiff black horsehair and is tied under the chin. It is called a *kat* (gaht). These hats are almost never seen today, but older Korean men usually wear a hat of some kind.

Traditional clothing for Korean women includes a long, loose, flowing skirt worn high above the waist and a very short, flared, long-sleeved blouse that crosses in front and ties with long colorful ribbons.

Today many people in South Korea wear Western-style clothing, especially in the cities. In North Korea, many wear plain clothes that look like uniforms. Throughout Korea, men are less likely than women to put on traditional clothes, even for ceremonies. But still, it is common in the cities and in the countryside to see people dressed in the old way.

5 다섯

(TAH-sut)

The pagoda of Pŏpchu-sa Temple (BOPE-choo-sa) has **five** stories and is made of wood. It is thought to be the oldest wooden pagoda in Korea.

Pagodas are graceful buildings that are like churches. They were first built in Korea when the religion called Buddhism came to the country in A.D. 372. Buddhism started in India, but China helped to spread it to Korea and other parts of the Far East.

Pŏpchu-sa Temple was built in A.D. 553. The five-story pagoda contains Korea's tallest statue of Buddha, or "Enlightened One."

XXIII 1984
XXIII 1984
XXIII 1984

6 여섯

(YEH-sut)

South Korea won **six** gold medals at the 1984 Summer Olympic Games in Los Angeles: one in women's archery, one in boxing, two in judo, and two in wrestling.

Of these sports, archery and judo are the two that have been popular in Korea for many centuries. Boxing and wrestling were not introduced until this century. Soccer and baseball are the most popular sports in Korea today.

The 1988 Summer Olympic Games were held in Seoul, the capital of South Korea. Only once before had an Asian nation, Japan, hosted the Olympics.

7 일곱

(ill-GUP)

There are **seven** types of pieces in the board game called *changgi* (CHONG-gee), which is a Korean kind of chess game. The game's two players each have one general, two chariots, two horses, two cannons, two elephants, two palace guards, and five soldiers. The object of the game is to capture the general.

Several other board games are popular in Korea. One, called *paduk* (BAH-dook), is a war game played with white and black stones. Old men often play these games on sidewalk boards or on park benches.

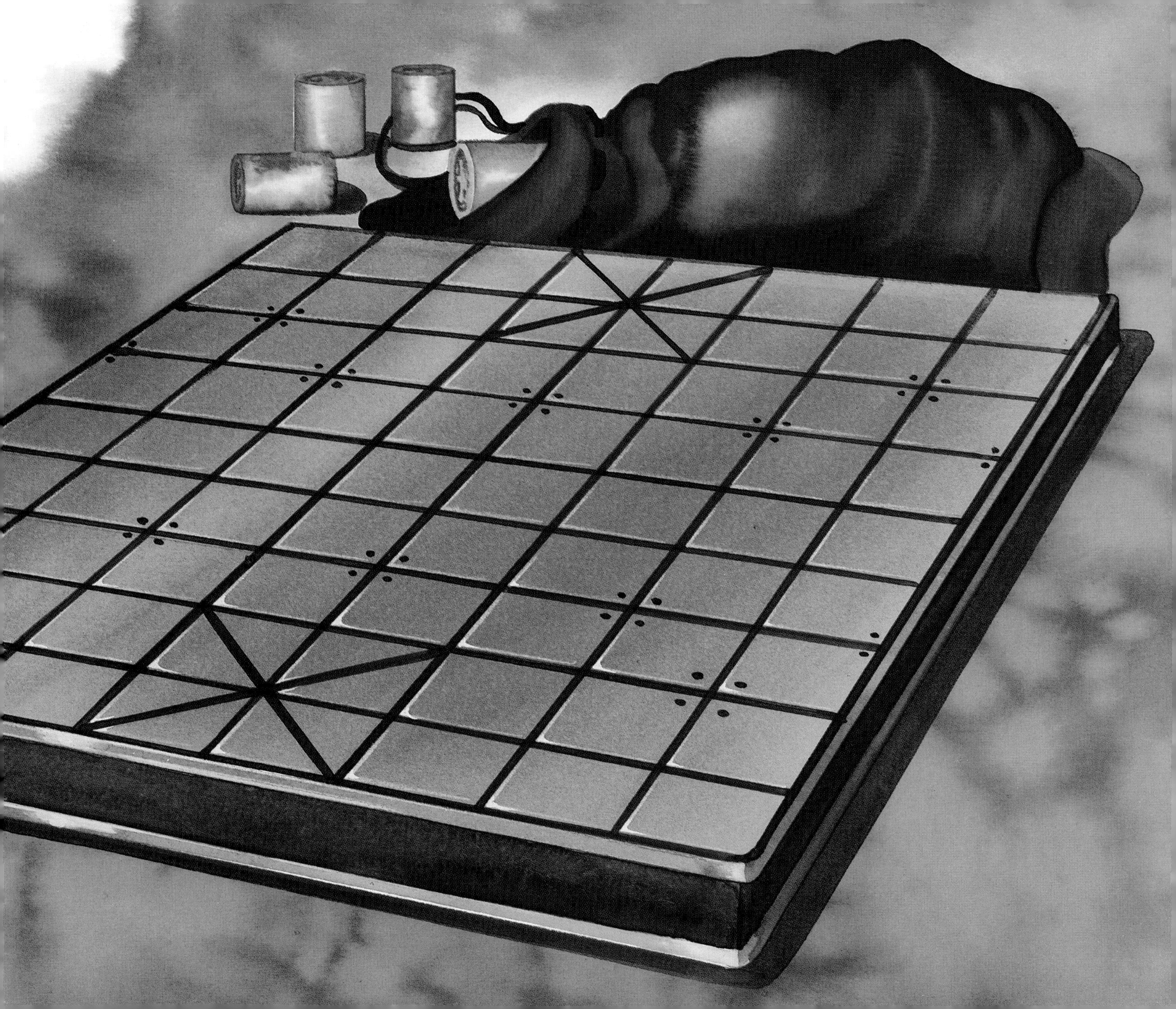

8 여덟

(yeh-DUL)

Eight kinds of seasonings are likely to be found at a Korean meal: red pepper, red pepper paste, soy sauce, soybean paste, ginger, garlic, sesame oil, and sesame seeds.

Much Korean food has a very spicy taste. Strong, hot foods are more common in Korean cooking than in Japanese or most Chinese dishes.

Another difference between Korean food and that of Japan and China is that in Korea a meal is not served one course at a time. Instead, all the dishes in a meal are served together.

9 아홉

(AH-hope)

There are **nine** players on a baseball team. Baseball is almost as popular in Korea as it is in the United States. It was introduced in 1906 to Korea by YMCA (Young Men's Christian Association) workers at the German Language Institute in Seoul.

The first Korean professional baseball league was formed in 1982. That year, South Korea won the 27th World Baseball Championship, which happened to be played in Seoul.

ㅏ A
ㅑ Ya
ㅜ U
ㅠ Yu
ㅡ Ŭ

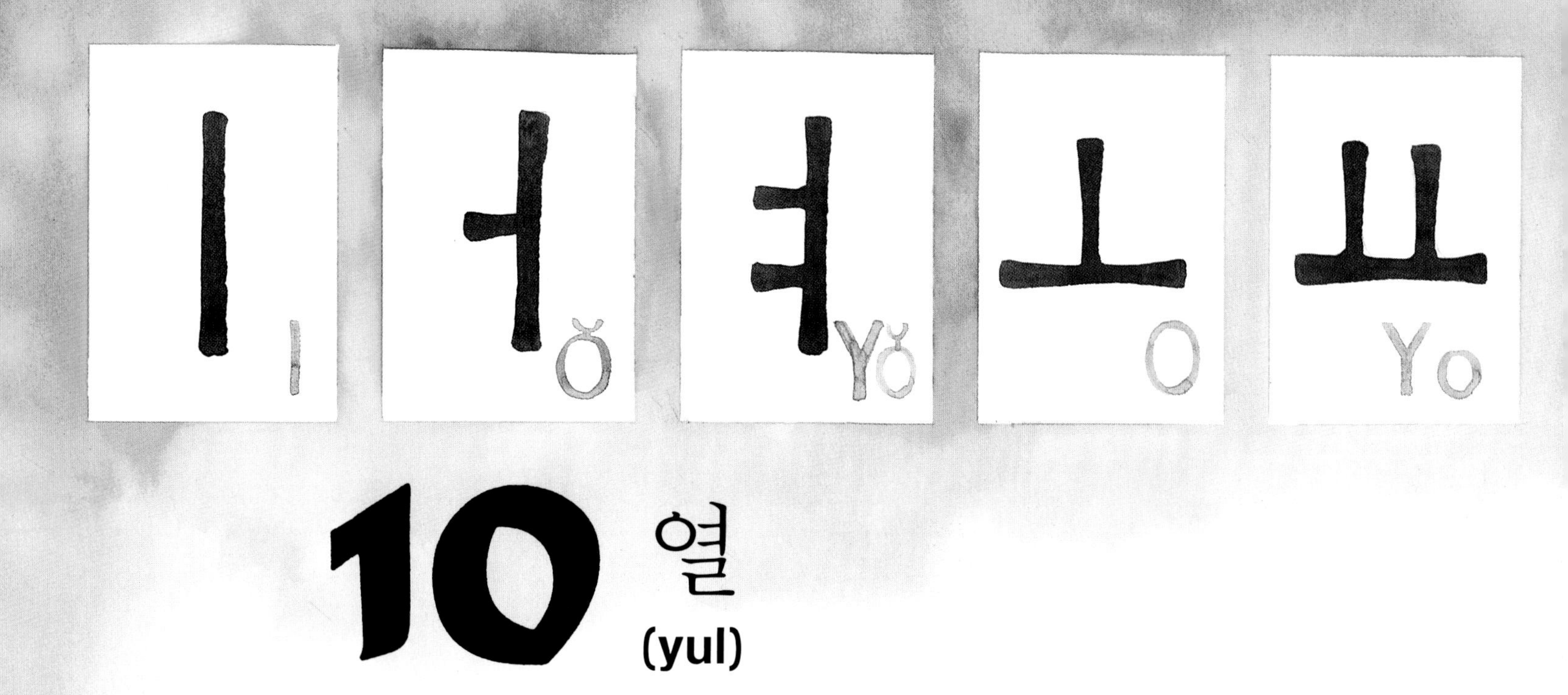

10 열 (yul)

There are **ten** vowels in the Korean alphabet, which is called *han-gŭl* (HONG-ol). Koreans are very proud of their alphabet.

Before the invention of their own alphabet during the 1400s, Koreans used Chinese characters for writing. These were hard to learn, and only the rulers and the wealthy had the time and money to learn how to write them. Then King Sejong the Great, who ruled Korea from 1418 to 1450, asked a group of scholars to develop a system of writing "for the people." *Han-gŭl* was the result.

Han-gŭl is easy to use in printing and in typewriting. Koreans believe that due to *han-gŭl*, their country has one of the highest literacy rates in the world: almost every Korean can read and write.

Pronunciation Guide

1 / 하나 / hah-NAH
2 / 둘 / tool
3 / 셋 / set
4 / 넷 / net
5 / 다섯 / TAH-sut
6 / 여섯 / YEH-sut
7 / 일곱 / ill-GUP
8 / 여덟 / yeh-DUL
9 / 아홉 / AH-hope
10 / 열 / yul